① Rice & funnel — fill jars with rice.

② fill jars with colored water — &
(draw marker lines to indicate
to show how far to fill up ja.

③ Have food containers — have kids sort items
in grocery bags according to catagories —
A paper goods   milk ⑤ alphabetical items
cleaning supplies   read label — first
bread   letter.
C. liquids — solids

ANIMAL MATH

④ Variety of pictures on different colored background.
sort: red animals — foods — flowers
        blue animals — foods — flowers

⑤ trace shapes of things on large paper —
students match items —
    ⓔ a ruler, a key, a book, a plate
can ask — what goes here? (use pens)

⑥ place items in box, bag or put sock over
container — student puts in hand & feels —
"what's in the box" — ⓔ spoon, brush, car, toy

ANIMAL MATH

ELLEN KELLER

Cuisenaire Company of America, Inc.
White Plains, New York

Cover photograph: Rob Gray
Cover design: Leslie Bauman
Text design and production: Leslie Bauman and Molly Heron
Illustrations: Mena Dolobowsky
Line art: Kay Wanous
Concept/Development: Judith Adams

Copyright © 1995 by
Cuisenaire Company of America, Inc.
PO Box 5026, White Plains, New York 10602

All rights reserved
Printed in the United States of America
ISBN 0-938587-81-1

Permission is granted for limited reproduction of pages from this book
for classroom use.

Table of Contents

Introduction 7

Counting with Animals 11

Animal Countdown 14

Animal Grab Bag 15

Estimating and Counting 16

Pick a Card 17

Animal Magic Squares 18

Sorting and Classifying with Animals 19

Animal Sorting 22

Guess My Rule 23

Sorting into Two Groups 24

Animal Facts 25

The Great Animal Switch 26

Using Venn Diagrams 27

Patterning with Animals 29

Adding to Patterns 31

What Is Missing? 32

Big and Little 33

Pattern Cards 34

Balancing and Weighing with Animals 35

Balancing 38

Making Dough Balls 39

Dough Balls Guessing Game 40

Heavy or Light? 41

Weighing Animal Groups 42

Telling Math Stories with Animals 43

The Far North 46

Animal Bazaar 47

The Animal Kingdom 48

Two Ticky Tales 49

Finding Strategies with Animals 51

Crocodile. 54

Barnyard Roundup 55

The Monkey Hop 56

Jungle Parade 57

The Great Race 58

Back in the Barnyard 59

Lions and Elephants 60

Building Fences 61

Telling More Math Stories 63

African Night 65

The Magic Jar 66

The Barnyard Mystery 67

Crossing the River 68

Big Animal Cutouts 69

Small Animal Cutouts 71

Introduction

ABOUT *ANIMAL MATH*

Animal Math is a collection of activities that allows children to work interactively with each page and with the animal pieces. These learning experiences offer a compelling and satisfying way for children in grades K through 2 to work with basic math concepts while solving problems and sharpening their thinking abilities. *Animal Math* also provides children with abundant opportunities for reading, writing, and communicating with others. All of these skills are consistent with the standards set forth in *Curriculum Standards and Evaluation for School Mathematics* published by the National Council of Teachers of Mathematics.

Each set of plastic animals consists of 40 domestic and 40 wild animal pieces. There are 5 varieties of domestic animals—cows, horses, pigs, sheep, and camels—4 big and 4 little of each. There are 10 varieties of wild animals—elephants, giraffes, polar bears, rhinoceroses, crocodiles, lions, moose, seals, hippopotamuses, and monkeys—2 big and 2 little of each.

The 36 activities in this book are organized into clusters based on mathematical concepts important to young children. The clusters are *Counting, Sorting and Classifying, Patterning, Balancing and Weighing, Telling Math Stories, Finding Strategies,* and *Telling More Math Stories.* These clusters and the activities within each cluster may be used in any order, but they fall into a natural sequence from more basic to more difficult.

Each cluster begins with Teachers Notes and is followed by corresponding student activity pages. The activity pages are open-ended and thus can (and should) be used more than once. The Teachers Notes give overviews of the activities and suggestions for how children can get the most out of them. Suggestions include discussion prompts, journal-writing opportunities, and links to trade books about animals. Often, Going Further sections provide extension ideas.

Since this book is intended for use by children across the primary grades, there will be substantial differences in reading abilities. Whereas some will be able to read all of the activity pages for themselves, you will probably have to read the pages to or with other children.

USING THE ANIMALS

Children respond with surprise and excitement when they first see the animal pieces. Give your children ample time to hold the animals, stand them up, pass them around, comment on favorites, and speculate on what they might be used for. Plan on several special occasions over a one- or two-week period during which individuals, pairs, and small groups can interact with the animals in any way they choose. Some will group the animals according to size or color. Others will string them across the entire room, invent animal scenarios or games, or simply share what they know about animals of each type. It is important that all children be able to use these animals in their own way before they are asked to focus on the activities in the book.

Make sure children understand that the relative size and colors of the animal pieces are not always realistic. For example, the large rhinoceros is smaller than the large lion; this

© 1995 Cuisenaire Company

would not be true of a real adult rhinoceros in relation to an adult lion. You may want to refer to library books as you discuss points such as this with children.

How children arrange themselves to work on the activity pages is largely up to you and will be partly determined by your supply of animal pieces. Although some pages specify that children work with a partner, children can usually do the same activity alone or with a small group. However, working together—sharing, considering, working things out— can be a most enriching experience.

As another option, you may choose to set up centers in your classroom with the animal pieces and any additional materials that children might need for the activities.

However your children work, they will get the most benefit from the activities if you gather the class together afterwards so that work and strategies can be shared.

Some pages are designed so that children can use them as workmats; others are not. Always encourage children to expand onto large surfaces such as other paper, table tops, or the floor. Similarly, when children record their work, make available lots of big sheets of paper so that children can think expansively. Children should use any method they like for recording. You might point out the pleasure to be had in figuring this out for oneself. Both as a recording option and as a way to add needed animal pieces, two pages of animal pictures (big and little) are provided for you to reproduce. You will find these at the back of this book.

For easy storage, keep the animal pieces in resealable plastic bags or in plastic tubs with tight lids. Since you will probably have more than one set of animals, you might store each set in a separate bag within the tub to simplify distribution to groups. The large bag or tub may also be used for activities in which children are asked to pick handfuls of assorted animals.

MAKING CONNECTIONS

Keeping Track of Animal Facts   One way to encourage children to gather more information about the real animals the pieces represent is to keep a language experience chart or wall log of pertinent information your children gather. To launch this, you might want to ask a question such as, "What are the different coverings the various animals can have?" Children will most likely suggest some. By examining photographs in books that you make available to them, children then will pick up even more information—for example, scales, skin, and so on. Support children as they pose questions of their own. Questions will occur again and again in children's conversations as they work with the activity pages and go on to invent their own activities and stories.

Animal Journals   Capitalize on the enthusiasm your children display by helping them make a journal for writing and drawing. Such a journal has many uses. For one thing, children can record experiences they have with the animal pieces. Open-ended problem-solving tasks such as those in *Animal Math* can begin with frustration for some children and end in joy when they "get it." Children can also write new information they have gleaned about the real animals that correspond to their pieces. They can use their journals to create or record animal stories, problems, games, and so on. Much that will go into the journals should be motivated by children's own impulses.

Let children choose their own physical type of journal. Some may want to construct a journal by stapling together several pieces of paper. Others may want to use notebooks.

© 1995 Cuisenaire Company

What is important is for children to feel that their journals are a personal expression of their experiences and ideas.

Literature and Animals   Your children should have frequent opportunities to locate information about the real animals these manipulatives represent. Children can help you find books for the class that have especially informative photographs, illustrations, captions, and information on specific animals. You should also provide books such as those listed below and other resources such as magazines, encyclopedias, museum brochures, posters, and so forth.

Bibliography   The non-fiction books listed in this bibliography, as well as many others in your library, will provide interesting information for your children to share.

Arnold, Caroline. *Elephant.* Morrow Jr. Books, 1993.

Cousteau Society. *Crocodiles and Alligators.* Marboro Books, 1988.

Dorros, Arthur. *Elephant Families.* "Let's Read and Find Out." HarperCollins, 1994.

Earle, Olive L. *Pigs Tame and Wild.* Morrow Jr. Books, 1959.

Greenaway, Theresa. *Amazing Bears.* "Eyewitness Juniors." Knopf, 1992.

Farm Animals. "Eye Openers." Macmillan/Dorling Kindersley, 1991.

Hopf, Alice. *Biography of a Rhino.* Putnam's, 1972.

Jacobsen, Karen. *Farm Animals.* "A New True Book." Children's Press, 1981.

Johnston, G. & J. Cutchins. *Scaly Babies, Reptiles Growing Up.* Morrow Jr. Books, 1988.

Leen, Nina. *Monkeys.* Holt, Rinehart and Winston, 1978.

Lumley, Kathryn Wentzel. *Monkeys and Apes.* "A New True Book." Children's Press, 1982.

Patent, Dorothy Hinshaw. *What Good Is a Tail?* Cobblehill Books/Dutton, 1994.

Patent, Dorothy Hinshaw. *Seals, Sea Lions, and Walruses.* Holiday House, 1990.

Rue, Leonard Lee III with William Own. *Meet the Moose.* Dodd, Mead & Company, 1985.

Schlein, Miriam. *Jane Goodall's Animal World: Hippos.* Atheneum, 1990.

Wallwork, Amanda. *No Dodos, A Counting Book of Endangered Animals.* Scholastic, 1993.

Yoshida, Toshi. *Young Lions.* Philomel, 1989.

Counting with Animals

Children learn to count in meaningful contexts. The activities in this cluster provide a variety of such counting experiences using animal pieces. Children are asked to notice particular characteristics of the pieces and then count how many times they occur among the animals (for example, how many animals have external ears). They discover for themselves, by counting, how many pieces are in the set, use the pieces for estimating, and play absorbing games that require counting.

As background for these counting activities, you might give children experiences creating and comparing groups with one-to-one correspondence, counting with cardinal numbers, and skip counting.

ANIMAL COUNTDOWN   (PAGE 14)

Overview Children identify, chart, and count physical characteristics shared by the animal pieces.

Before Before you show children the activity page, you might draw a chart of columns on the chalkboard like the one on the activity page. Under each column, name a physical characteristic or item of clothing shared by children in the class; for example, brown eyes or red shirts. Choose volunteers to record with tally marks on the board whatever they see—each pair of brown eyes or each red shirt. Have children count the number of each characteristic.

Since this is the first activity page, generate interest in the book by having children look at it together. Suggest that if they need a larger workspace, they can use a bigger sheet of paper. Tell children that this and all the pages can be used over again in different ways and that they may work alone or with others. Be sure to make library books available to any children who want to find additional information about the animals.

After Children may have noticed a wide variety of characteristics, including fur, horns, tails, long necks, legs, and so on. Give them an opportunity to share their findings and to compare and recount totals. Ask children to describe how they collected and counted their data. Some children may have counted by 1s, 2s and 4s; others only by 1s. If children gathered information for this activity from books, suggest that they share some of what they learned with the class. Encourage children to use their journals for writing and drawing about what they discovered.

Going Further Challenge children to find a way to display the data and compare the characteristics and numbers for different animals. If they decide to show picture or bar graphs, they can use the animal cutouts on pages 69 and 71 to represent the different animals.

ANIMAL GRAB BAG   (PAGE 15)

Overview Children use sketches, tally marks, and other symbols to record groups of animals and then the entire set.

© 1995 Cuisenaire Company

Before Before beginning, ask children how they would record their handfuls. Review making tally marks. First show how to make one vertical mark for each item counted and then model how to make groups of 5 with 4 vertical and one horizontal or diagonal mark.

After Ask children to describe the different ways they recorded the animals.
   As part of a discussion, use key questions such as these:
   • Did you pick about the same number of animals each time? How can you tell?
   • Which handful had the most animals? The fewest?
   • How can two numbers be the same if the recordings look different?
   • Which animal was picked most often?

Going Further Children can explore *Anno's Counting Book* by M. Anno (Crowell, 1977) as well as other counting books. Some may want to create a similar big book illustrating different numbers of domestic or wild animals, or the entire set.

ESTIMATING AND COUNTING   (PAGE 16)

Overview Children estimate numbers of animals and count to check their estimates.

Before Discuss with children the meaning of the word *estimate*, first as a verb and then as a noun. Give an example using classroom items such as books on a shelf. Introduce the concept of estimating by asking children questions such as "How many children do you think could walk through the door at the same time?" "Why do you think so?" Point out that an estimate is a "good guess" based on careful thinking.

After Encourage pairs or groups to tell the class about their estimates and say whether they got better as they went along. Discuss what "fit" means. When children checked their estimates, did they place the animals nose to tail or sideways? Did they leave space between the animals? Have children consider how their placement of the animal pieces affected their results.

PICK A CARD   (PAGE 17)

Overview Children practice counting by following directions on game cards and then write and follow directions of their own.

Before Depending on your group, you may want to read the game directions together and talk about how the game is played. Especially toward the end of the game, you may want to allow children to take fewer animals than the card directs them to take. For instance, if the card says to take 4 animals of one kind and there are only 3 animals of one kind left, you can guide children to take the 3. If this is not allowed, the game is more of a challenge, requiring more strategy.

After Encourage children to share the strategies they used to play (and possibly win) the game. Some possible strategies are to make groups of wild animals first, since they are smaller groups to begin with; to not take any animals that your partner is already collecting; or whenever possible to try and take animals that are complete groups or will complete a group. Children can record these strategies in their journals.

© 1995 Cuisenaire Company

ANIMAL MAGIC SQUARES   (PAGE 18)

Overview Children create a magic square by placing animals in spaces so that they add up to 10 in each row, column, and diagonal.

Before To fully understand the directional terms *across*, *down*, and *diagonal*, younger children might need some experience working with a magic square before they begin. If you like, draw a magic-square outline with 3 rows across and 3 columns down. Ask children to put Xs on the diagonals going from the upper left corner down to the lower right corner, and do the same thing for the other diagonal. Other volunteers could draw a line across each row and down each column.

After As part of a discussion, use key questions such as these:
- How did you go about filling your magic square?
- What strategy did you use to make 10 each time?
- Was any part hard? If so, why?

Going Further Children who are ready might repeat the activity using numbers without pictures. Some children may want to create a magic-square game board on which they fill in some of the squares with animal drawings and give the game board to a friend to complete. They could also make 3 x 3 magic squares that add up to 15.

© 1995 Cuisenaire Company

Animal Countdown

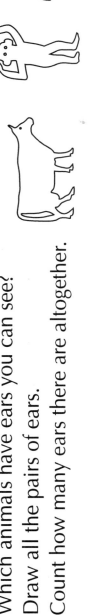

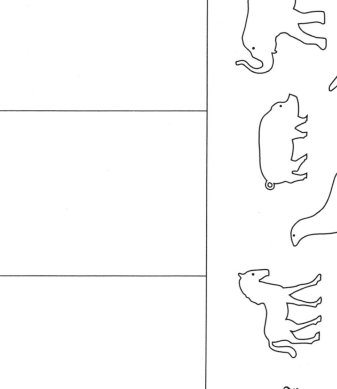

Put out one animal of each kind.
Which animals have ears you can see?
Draw all the pairs of ears.
Count how many ears there are altogether.

ears

What is something else some animals have?
Add that word to the chart next to "ears."
Draw each one of these that you see.
Count how many there are altogether.

Find more things to show on the chart.
What does the chart tell you?

© 1995 Cuisenaire Company

Counting   ANIMAL MATH
© 1995 Cuisenaire Company

Animal Grab Bag

Work with a partner.
Put all your animals into a bag.
Take turns grabbing all the animals
you can with one hand.
Record all the animals in each handful.
Group your drawings or marks
so that they are easy to count.
Put the animals back in the bag each time.

First handful

Second handful

Third handful

Compare your handfuls with your partner's.
Empty the bag on the table.
Count how many animals there are altogether.

© 1995 Cuisenaire Company

Estimating and Counting

Work with a partner.
Spill all your animals into a big container.
How many can you scoop out with two hands?
One of you scoops and the other guesses how many.
Count to see if the estimate was close.
Try this several times.

	Estimate	Number
1.		
2.		
3.		
4.		

Choose one kind of big barnyard animal.
How many do you think will fit on this line? Estimate.
Use animals to see if your estimate was close.

_____

Estimate how many of that same animal will fit on each of these lines.
Use animals to check your estimates.

_____

_____

_____

Tell your partner how to make good estimates.

© 1995 Cuisenaire Company

Pick a Card

Play with a partner.
Use all your animals.

Cut out the cards.
Stack them face down.
Turn one over.

To win this game, you must have
more animal groups than your partner.
• A group is all the big and little animals
  of one kind.

To play, take turns with your partner.
• Pick a card and read it out loud.
• Take the animals you need.
• Put the card face down in a new stack.
• Tally to record each complete group.
• Play until all the animals are taken.

Play the game again.
Add more cards with your
own rules on them.

Take 4 animals of one kind.

Take 2 animals of one kind
and 3 different animals.

Take 1 animal.

Take 4 animals of one kind
and 3 of another kind.

Take any number of one
kind of animal.

Take any number of one
kind of animal and 3 of
another kind.

Take no animals.

Take 3 different animals.

Take all the animals you
need to complete 1 group.

Take 4 big and 4 little
animals of the same kind.

Take 3 animals of one kind.

Animal Magic Squares

Look at the first row across.
Put 1, 2, 3, or 4 little animals in the empty square.
Make the first row add up to 10 animals.
Put little animals in the other empty squares.
Each row across and each column down must add up to 10 animals.
All the diagonals must add up to 10, too.

Compare your Animal Magic Squares with a classmate's.

Start again.
Make your own animal grid.
Put animals in each square to make 10.

Counting ANIMAL MATH
© 1995 Cuisenaire Company

Sorting and Classifying with Animals

Sorting and classifying are activities that children engage in as a matter of course in their everyday lives as they identify and group things in their world. The animal pieces are especially good manipulatives for sorting and classifying activities because they have such a variety of characteristics.

Children are likely to classify the animals by physical characteristics and by other attributes as well. Give children ample time to investigate the animals. They will soon discover and search for such physical attributes as fur, tusks, horns, leg and tail length, color, and size. Children may notice that some of the animal pieces have a seam down their backs or a notch in the plastic on the neck. These manufacturing details, along with others, can also be used for classification purposes. Encourage children to look beyond the physical. Habitat, diet, and value to human beings are just a few of the nonphysical ways in which children may group the animals.

ANIMAL SORTING   (PAGE 22)

Overview Children sort their animal pieces in an open-ended activity. They group handfuls of animals and then resort each other's groups in a different way.

Before With younger children, you may want to be sure they are comfortable with simple sorting activities before they work with the animal pieces. For example, sorting materials with different shapes, colors, or sizes provides good preparation for sorting animal pieces.

After Give children an opportunity to share and compare their findings.
   As part of a discussion, use key questions such as these:
   • How many different ways can you sort the animals you picked? What are some of the ways to sort?
   • What did you think about as you decided how to sort the animal pieces into groups?
   • What are some of the ways you could record your groups?

Going Further Challenge children to put their sorted groups in horizontal or vertical graphing grids.

GUESS MY RULE   (PAGE 23)

Overview Animals are sorted according to one attribute and placed in a circle while all others are placed outside the loop. Children identify which animals belong together in some way and which do not.

Before To prepare children to distinguish between things that go inside a loop and things that do not, place a circular object like a hula-hoop on the floor. Put inside the loop three books whose covers show that they are about animals; outside the loop, put two books that obviously have nothing to do with animals. Encourage children to discuss what they

© 1995 Cuisenaire Company

see. Ask them to guess the sorting rule by adding items inside and outside the loop. Children can then explain why some books are outside the loop.

After Discuss the possible sorting rules for the animals pictured inside the circle (for example, animals with horns or tusks or animals with hoofs). Encourage children to share the thinking that led to their rules and their selection of animal pieces to go inside. As children demonstrate some of their groupings, have others tell whether the same grouping can be described differently. Discuss attributes that the animals share, possibly looking in reference books for pictures and photographs that give ideas for sorting.

SORTING INTO TWO GROUPS (PAGE 24)

Overview Children sort the animals into two groups by identifying the sorting rules and extending the groups.

Before You might want to lay the groundwork for the notion of sorting into two groups. One way is to help children sort themselves into two groups, those with birthdays between January and June and those with birthdays between July and December. Make two headings on the chalkboard and survey children until you have recorded everyone's birthday in one place or the other.

After Children may discover that there is often more than one way to describe the same group of animals; that there is sometimes more than one way to sort the same group of animals into two groups; that the two groups may be related in that they have to do with differences in the same attributes (for example, big and little relate to size). Some children may also discover that one grouping of animals can go into both loops. Explain that this is indeed true.

Ask children to talk about the animals they grouped with the little polar bear and the big elephant. Invite them to share their process of deciding on their two categories. Also encourage children to respond to their classmates' choices. Some of the ways children may have classified the animals are white and gray, big and little, those that live in the cold, icy north and those that live in the jungle, those with short or long tails, and those with or without tusks or horns.

ANIMAL FACTS (PAGE 25)

Overview Children identify the attributes of some animals and use that information to sort into two intersecting loops.

Before You might begin a discussion in which children consider how they could describe themselves by two attributes. For example, a child might be a girl with brown hair. After some children have contributed, put two loops on the floor. Ask all the girls to stand in one loop and all the children with brown hair to stand in the other loop. Ask where boys with brown hair should go. Without pushing children, give them the chance to notice that such a sorting might present a problem.

© 1995 Cuisenaire Company

After Allow time for children to share the different groupings that they created. Ask them what they noticed about sorting one animal by two attributes. Help children to explain why the animals that can go in both loops belong in the overlapping area of the two loops.

THE GREAT ANIMAL SWITCH   (PAGE 26)

Overview Children sort the animal pieces into two overlapping loops according to explicit rules or categories. One child moves a few animals from one area to the other, and the partner identifies those that were moved.

Before *The Elephant's Wish* by Bruno Munari (World, 1959) is a good book to read to children before they begin the activity. After each spread, stop so that children can compare attributes of each animal and the animal it wishes to be. Children may prefer to make large sorting loops on the floor rather than reusing the loops on the page.

After Discuss which pairs of cutout labels children selected. Then have volunteers describe their thinking as they worked out the activity. As part of a discussion, ask key questions such as these:
  • What is the middle area for?
  • Why do some animals fit in the middle?
Some children may want to record their thoughts about this activity in their journals.

Going Further Pairs of children might like to sort their animals into three groups instead of two. They can either build on the given pairs of sorting rules or make up all their own sorting rules. Either way, suggest that after they sort, children switch some of the animals from one group to another for someone else to identify.

USING VENN DIAGRAMS   (PAGE 27)

Overview Children classify and sort the animal pieces into two overlapping loops by following the rules.

Before Some children may have difficulty working backwards, that is, naming the loops when they know the intersection. Give these children pairs of labels such as the ones used in *Animal Facts*. Place two loops on the floor. Ask a child to place a label on each loop. Then make a special label for the intersection, pointing out that both attributes are in the new label. Do this several times.

After Make sure children understand that there is more than one way to sort the same animals. Be clear with children that you expect them to be able to explain how they think as they work. As part of a discussion, ask a key question such as this:
  • How did you choose the sorting rule for each unlabelled area?

© 1995 Cuisenaire Company

Animal Sorting

Put all your animals in a bag.
Grab two big handfuls.
Sort the animals into different groups.
Think of a good name for each group.
Share what you did with a partner.

Mix up your animals.
Change places with your partner.
Try to sort your partner's animals
into new groups.

Check each other's work.
Talk about it with your partner.

Find a way to record some of your groups here.

Sorting and Classifying ANIMAL MATH

© 1995 Cuisenaire Company

Guess My Rule

This circle holds animals that are alike in some way.

Why do you think the animals might belong together?

Can you add more animals that belong?

Work with a partner.
Make a loop on the table with yarn or string.

One of you gathers some animals
that go together and puts them inside the loop.
Put some animals that do not belong outside.
The other person guesses the rule for the loop and
adds more animals that belong.

Keep playing "Guess My Rule."

© 1995 Cuisenaire Company

Sorting into Two Groups

Each loop is for animals that belong together.

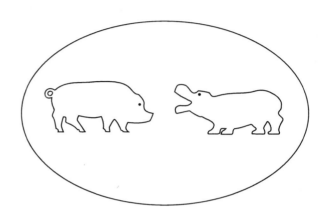

Think of a rule for the second loop.
Write your rule on the line.
Add animals to each loop.

Make up rules for each of these loops.
Add animals that fit your rules.

Choose a partner.
Compare rules.
Together, make all the two-loop sorts you can.

Sorting and Classifying   ANIMAL MATH

© 1995 Cuisenaire Company

Animal Facts

Work with a partner.
List facts about the seal on another paper.
List what you see and what you know.
Use two facts to write rules for the loops.
Where does your seal belong?
Add more animals to each of the areas.

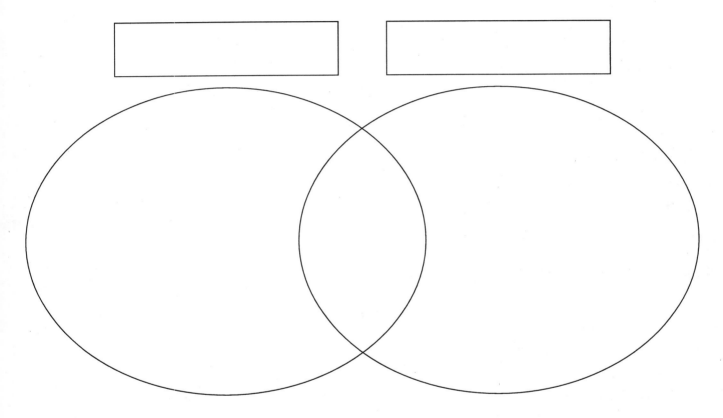

Draw new loops like those above.
Use these pairs of labels to sort some of your animals.

Farm animals	Wild animals	Likes cold	Has mane
White animals	Big animals	Likes water	Shade of brown

© 1995 Cuisenaire Company

The Great Animal Switch

Work with a partner using all your animals.
Read the sorting rules.
Sort your animals into the two groups.

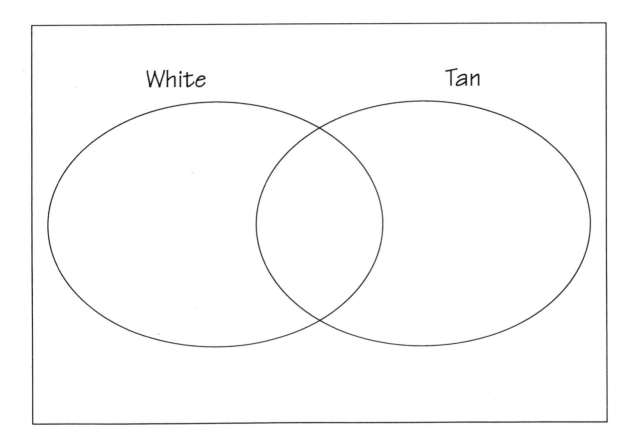

White   Tan

Close your eyes.
Your partner switches some animals into another area.
Which animals are in the wrong area?

Cut out the pairs of labels on this page.
Put the labels over the rules for the two loops.
Follow the new rules to sort your animals.

Play the switching game again with your partner.

Use all the labels in the same way.

Sorting and Classifying   ANIMAL MATH
© 1995 Cuisenaire Company

Eats animals

Eats plants

Long legs

Short legs

People run from

People ride on

Likes hot

Likes cold

Using Venn Diagrams

Work with a partner.
Place all your animals on the table.
Make overlapping loops.

Think of a rule for the other loop.
Put animals where they belong.
Put any animals that fit both rules
into the middle.

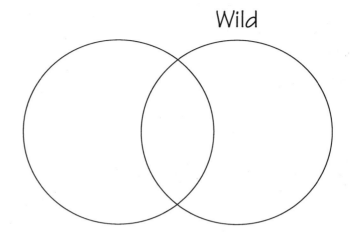

Do the same thing
with these two new loops.

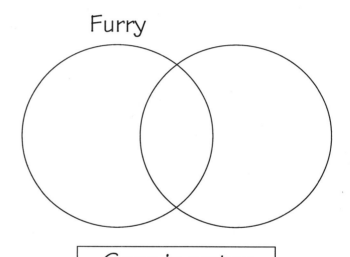

Think about the rule in the middle.
Which two rules could fit the loops?
Sort some animals into the loops and
into the overlapping part.

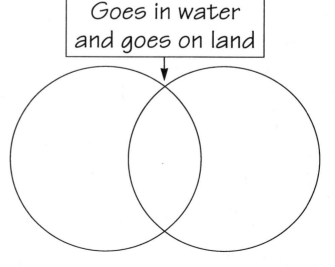

© 1995 Cuisenaire Company

Patterning with Animals

Before beginning the patterning activities, ask children to talk about what they think a pattern is. There are many patterns around us that children may have observed in nature, in clothing designs, and in architecture (for example, in bridges). If possible, show children patterns of the sort made by the repeated segments of a necklace or around a cup or other piece of pottery. Most children have created patterns in arts and crafts activities and when building with blocks. Invite them to describe such experiences.

ADDING TO PATTERNS   (PAGE 31)

Overview Children are given patterns to identify and extend.

Before Before beginning, explain that children can make and record these patterns any way they like. They might use the animal pieces, draw pictures of the animals, write the animal names, or use pictures cut out of magazines or from pages 69 and 71 of this book.

After Ask children to identify the first pattern in their own words. Then have them share their original patterns with the class. Encourage discussion about what factors come into play in creating animal patterns.

WHAT IS MISSING?   (PAGE 32)

Overview Children create animal patterns, remove some animals, and ask other children to complete their patterns.

Before For those children who might find it difficult to supply a missing element in a pattern, draw a repeated pattern based on three animals. Have children describe the basic pattern. Erase one element and ask a child to tell you or to draw in what is missing. Do this a few times with different three-element patterns.

Have children compare patterns to determine how they are the same and how they are different. Suggest that children look at color and size of the animals used, the type(s) of animal used, the position(s) of the animals, how many times the sequence repeats, how many animals are in the sequence, and so on.

BIG AND LITTLE   (PAGE 33)

Overview Using big and little animals of one kind, children create and record various pattern possibilities. They also copy patterns created by a partner and collaborate to make new patterns.

Before If necessary, give children an idea of possible linear patterns they can create with two elements. Use letters to show examples such as ABABAB, ABBABB, or AABAAB. You might also present the concept of growing patterns such as ABAABAAAB or ABAAB-BAAABBB.

After As part of a discussion, use key questions such as these:
  • Which animal did you choose for your big and little pattern?

© 1995 Cuisenaire Company

- Could someone use a different animal and make the same pattern?
- How many different big and little patterns do you think you could make?
- What different ways could you record your patterns?

Going Further Ask children what kinds of patterns they could create if they had three sizes of each animal—big, medium, and little. Challenge children to create patterns based on animals of three sizes and to display them for their classmates to see.

PATTERN CARDS   (PAGE 34)

Overview Children create and record different animal patterns to fit the same specifications.

Before To provide an engaging context for children's exploration, have them pretend that they just started a business in which they create and draw different animal pattern designs. Explain that these designs may be used on animal posters, book covers, or clothing. Challenge pairs of children to use the animals and one of the pattern cards to create as many patterns as possible. Allow children to share their work and their process of creating the patterns.

After As part of a discussion, use key questions such as these:
- How many patterns did you make for each card?
- Which card direction was the easiest to work with? Which was the hardest? Why?
- Did color figure into any of your patterns? How?

Going Further Some children may want to create a game using pattern cards for the class. Talk about various card games and how they might be adapted to use patterns. "Concentration" could be one example.

© 1995 Cuisenaire Company

Adding to Patterns

Work with a partner.
Look at this pattern.

What could the pattern be?
Add more big animals to continue the pattern.

Each of you makes a new pattern with big animals.
Record your pattern here.

Switch papers.
Continue each other's patterns.
Talk with your partner about what you did.

© 1995 Cuisenaire Company

What is Missing?

Pick any 3 animals.

Arrange them in a row.

Add animals to repeat the pattern.

Record your pattern here.

Take away 1 or 2 animals.

Record the pattern you see now.

Switch papers with a classmate.

Decide what is missing from your classmate's pattern.

Complete the pattern.

Talk with your classmate about how you decided which animals you needed.

Repeat this activity with other animals.

© 1995 Cuisenaire Company

Big and Little

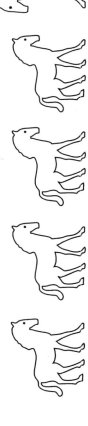

Find all the big and little animals of one kind.
Make a pattern with the animals.
Record your pattern here.

What other patterns can you make
with big and little?

Compare patterns with a classmate.
How are they alike? How are they different?
Try to make each other's patterns.
Work with your classmate to make a new patterns.

© 1995 Cuisenaire Company

Pattern Cards

Work with a partner.
Each of you chooses one pattern card at a time.
Follow the directions and make as many different patterns
as you can. Record all the patterns.

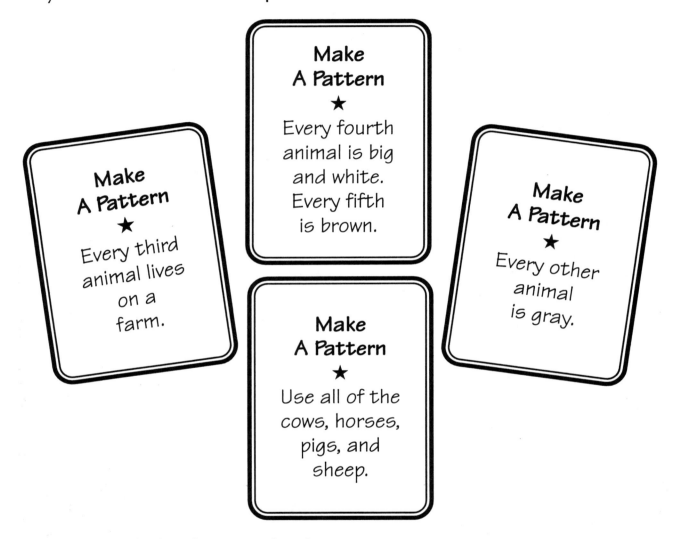

**Make
A Pattern**
★
Every third
animal lives
on a
farm.

**Make
A Pattern**
★
Every fourth
animal is big
and white.
Every fifth
is brown.

**Make
A Pattern**
★
Every other
animal
is gray.

**Make
A Pattern**
★
Use all of the
cows, horses,
pigs, and
sheep.

Which card helped you make the most patterns?
Why?

Invent more patterns with the animals.
Make more pattern cards.
You and your partner could make a whole deck.

© 1995 Cuisenaire Company

Balancing and Weighing with Animals

Balancing and weighing are measurement skills that children use when they compare themselves to others, build with blocks, and shop at the store, to name a few examples. In this cluster of activities, the children are given multiple experiences comparing the weights of animal pieces. This prepares them for subsequent work using standard and nonstandard units of measure. They develop a sense of weight by matching dough balls to animals and by identifying which animal or group of animals is lighter, heavier, or equivalent in weight to another. Encourage children to record their results by drawing pictures, tallying, writing addition exercises, or using the animal cutouts on pages 69 and 71.

If possible, try to use ready-made balance scales to check the children's work. For the most accurate results, use a simple rocker or primary balance scale that allows items to be placed in any location without affecting the accuracy or making the scale tip over. The scale should also be sensitive to slight weight changes, such as 1 gram, since the animals themselves are quite light to begin with. If you are so inclined, however, explore ways to make your own balance scale in the classroom. Use your creativity and any materials that are available to you, such as rulers, cups, modeling clay, wire hangers, string, and purchased or teacher-made fulcrums.

BALANCING   (PAGE 38)

Overview Children compare the weight of one animal with that of one or more other animals to determine equivalent weights.

Before Discuss what it means to balance something. Have children talk about balancing on a seesaw. It may also be helpful to set out the kind of scale children will use and model by balancing first two objects and then one object with two or more. Have children share their results. Before you begin, make sure children understand that the equal sign on the activity page means "is the same as."

After Some possible animals or groups of animals that weigh the same as 1 big elephant are 2 big lions; 1 big sheep, camel, horse, and cow; 1 big monkey, moose, and lion; 1 little and 4 big horses; 3 big pigs. Let children name the other animals they chose to balance and compare what they learned. Children can record their results in their journals by drawing pictures, using plus signs, gluing down animal cutouts, or writing sentences.

Going Further To make real-life connections for children, you may want to take them to a playground to actually explore balancing on a seesaw. Sit on one side of the seesaw and have combinations of children get on the other side to try to balance the beam.

MAKING DOUGH BALLS   (PAGE 39)

Overview Children figure out how to make dough balls whose weights are equivalent to the big animals. They make and then compare the dough balls with the animals they match.

ANIMAL MATH   Balancing and Weighing with Animals   **35**
© 1995 Cuisenaire Company

Before In preparation, set out the ingredients and other supplies needed to make the dough. Small paper cups will most likely be adequate for producing the amount of dough children will need. You may also want to provide food coloring to make the dough more attractive, but keep in mind that a small amount of color goes a long way. If the dough is too sticky, have children add a little more flour and/or salt to the mixture. Before children start working, suggest they devise a way to label the dough balls they make or to keep each animal and its dough ball together.

After Ask volunteers to explain how they decided what to do after the dough was ready. Some may have simply held an animal in one hand and a dough ball in the other, approximating equivalent weights. Others probably used a scale.

Have children compare the animals and their dough balls. Children who used a scale will probably notice that the size of a dough ball is related to the weight of its animal: The heavier an animal, the bigger the dough ball. (If children have difficulty understanding the relationship between an animal and a dough ball, have them imagine that each animal was melted down and the hot plastic was rolled into a ball.) Children who didn't use a scale will probably have gotten a variety of different results. At the end of the activity, give those children the opportunity to check their work on a scale before playing the Dough Balls Guessing Game on page 40. Make sure each pair of children puts its set of dough balls into a resealable plastic bag so it will be available for the next activity and won't dry out.

DOUGH BALLS GUESSING GAME (PAGE 40)

Overview Children use the dough balls they made in the last activity to play an estimation game. By looking at and holding dough balls and animals, children guess which dough ball and which big animal is equivalent in weight.

Before In preparation, make sure each pair of children has two sets of dough balls from the previous activity.

After As part of a discussion, use a key question such as this:
  • What strategies did you use to choose the dough balls?
  Challenge children to find a way to record the one or two dough balls they used to match the weight of the animals.

HEAVY OR LIGHT? (PAGE 41)

Overview Children estimate and order the weights of five animals by lifting them in pairs and checking their estimates on a scale.

Before To give children an opportunity to work with the concepts of heaviest, lightest, and weights in between, have them lift at least four books, of clearly different weights, two at a time, and place them on a table in order from heaviest to lightest. Encourage children to describe the weights using words such as *heaviest, lightest, next to lightest,* and so on.

© 1995 Cuisenaire Company

After As a part of a discussion, use key questions such as these:
- Did lifting the animals in pairs help you to guess which is heaviest? Why?
- How can you use the scale to check your guess?

Going Further This is an opportune time for children to do research in encyclopedias or other informational books to find out about animals' weights and how they are weighed. For example, an elephant may weigh as much as a car. An elephant trainer weighs an elephant by putting a right front leg on one scale and a left back leg on another scale. Challenge children to work in pairs to devise a method or device for weighing other animals. Children can then write about and draw their inventions in their animal journals.

WEIGHING ANIMAL GROUPS (PAGE 42)

Overview Using a balance scale, children compare the weights of animal groups using the language *heavier than*, *lighter than*, and *about the same as*.

Before Begin by reviewing with children how to read the chart on the activity page. For example, in the first row, children must find animals that are heavier than, lighter than, and weigh about the same as three big horses.

After After children share and compare results, discuss how the answers could be different and still be correct. Help children to understand that the same animal group could be heavier and lighter, depending on what it is being compared to. Let children express their thoughts about the question at the bottom of the page.

Going Further Invite children to make their own animal question, using the one at the bottom of the page as a model.

© 1995 Cuisenaire Company

Balancing

You will need a balance scale.
Put a big elephant on one side of the scale.

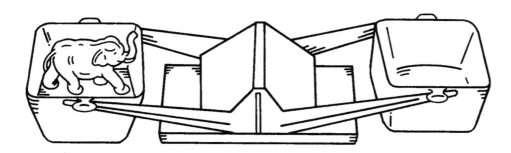

Which animals will balance the elephant?
Try using different animals or groups of animals.
Write about what you found out.

1 big elephant = _____

= _____

= _____

= _____

Pick another animal to balance on the scale.
Record what you discover on another paper.

Making Dough Balls

Make dough with a partner.
You will need

2 CUPS Flour   1 CUP Water   1 CUP Salt   1 Tablespoon Oil   Bowl

Mix the dough together.
Squeeze and roll the dough until it feels right.

Each of you makes a dough ball that is as heavy as each big animal.
Decide how to do this.

Compare your animals with their dough balls.
Talk with your partner about what you see and what you think.

© 1995 Cuisenaire Company

Dough Balls Guessing Game

Play this game with a partner.
Put all the big animals into a bag.
Each of you puts a set of dough balls on the table.

Take turns taking an animal from the bag. Find 1 or 2 dough balls that seem to weigh the same as your animal.

Use a scale to check your guess.

If your guess is right, you may keep the animal.
If not, put it back in the bag.

Play until all the animals have been picked.
Whoever has the most animals wins the game.

Balancing and Weighing   ANIMAL MATH
© 1995 Cuisenaire Company

Heavy or Light?

You will need a balance scale and animal pictures.
Put these animals on the table.

Which animal is the heaviest?
Which is the lightest?
Lift different pairs of animals and guess.
Use the seesaw to help you put them in order.
Use animal pictures to record your guesses.

Heaviest

Next to
Heaviest

Next
lighter

Next to
lighter

Next to
lightest

Lightest

Weigh the animals to check your guess.
Move animals if you need to.
Record what you learn.

Try this again with other big animals.

© 1995 Cuisenaire Company

Weighing Animal Groups

Put 3 big horses on a balance scale.
Which animal or animal groups are heavier?
Lighter? About the same?

Record what you find across the first row of the chart.
Continue across to complete the chart.
Add your own starting animals when you need to.

Starting Animals	These animals are heavier	These animals are lighter	These animals are about the same

Suppose 3 horses are lighter than 2 elephants.
Can 1 elephant be heavier than 3 horses?

Balancing and Weighing   ANIMAL MATH
© 1995 Cuisenaire Company

Telling Math Stories with Animals

When children play with the animal pieces, they often make up intricate stories about individual animals and groups of animals. Some of these stories may involve adding or taking away animals from a group. Building on this kind of activity, each math story in this cluster is, in effect, a specific situation that may be solved with the operation of addition and/or subtraction.

You will find that children use various methods and strategies to find solutions to these stories. Initially, they may use counting strategies such as counting on and counting back. Whatever methods they use, children should be encouraged to act out the problems with animal pieces directly on the pictures from the stories. Using manipulatives helps make a complex problem real and vivid.

Depending on the reading level of children in your class, you may want to read the stories in this cluster aloud as children follow along. Before reading each story, take full advantage of the illustrations to draw children in. Try not to direct the children to use a particular operation to solve the problem. Children may approach the same story in different ways, such as using counting up instead of counting on to find the number of animals in *Animal Bazaar*.

THE FAR NORTH   (PAGE 46)

Overview Children read a "story" set in the Far North and then add polar bears and seals to a picture to reflect the situation that is described. They choose a way to find the total number of animals in the picture.

Before Children will find it helpful but not necessary to have some experience solving basic addition facts using the strategies for counting up and counting back. To set the scene for the story, ask children to find the Far North on a wall map. Allow them to tell anything they know about the region, whether real or imaginary. Give children the activity page and encourage their responses. Tell children that the girl and the mother in the picture are called Inuits. Together with the children, create the mood for the story, where all is quiet except for the wind. If you like, have children imitate the sound of the wind as you read the story aloud.

After Children can share and compare answers to the story questions and the methods they used to find out. Have volunteers share the story they made up about the animals joining the group in the picture. Those children who are able to can write their stories in their animal journals. Some children might want to research seals and polar bears in the classroom or school library and add that information to their journals.

Going Further You might want to challenge children to write an addition exercise to find the total number of animals. By writing the same numbers in different ways, children may come to see that the order of the addends doesn't change the total.

© 1995 Cuisenaire Company

ANIMAL BAZAAR   (PAGE 47)

Overview Children read part of a story about animals at a bazaar and add elephants, horses, and camels to a picture to match numbers given. After they finish the story, they remove animals and find how many are left.

Before Ask children to look at the activity page and talk about it together. Explain to children that throughout the world, animals, food, clothing, and other items are often sold in outdoor markets called bazaars. Some children may be familiar with *bazaar* in another context. Let them tell what they know. Read the story aloud while children listen.

After As part of a discussion, use key questions such as these:
  • How did you figure out which animals to add to the picture?
  • How did using the animal pieces help you find how many animals were left?
  • Was any part of your work hard? Talk about that.
Give children time to tell how they changed the story.

THE ANIMAL KINGDOM   (PAGE 48)

Overview By acting out a story with a large number of animals, children add and subtract numbers to solve a problem.

Before If appropriate to your group, have children read the story silently. Ask how using the animal pieces might help children to understand the questions at the end of the story.

After If possible, read and show the picture book *1 Hunter* by Pat Hutchins (Greenwillow, 1982). This is a visual math puzzle in which animals are camouflaged in the art. Ask children to suggest ways in which they could find out the total number of animals that appear in the story. Pairs of children might use the animal pieces for the book animals to solve the problem. Others might suggest going through the book a second time and making a list of animals on the chalkboard.

Going Further As an interesting extension to the activity, have children work with partners to draw or find and cut out different groups of animals and mount them on one large sheet of paper. Challenge children to find out the total number of animals on the paper. You might give each pair several possible totals and have them decide whether each answer is reasonable and which seems closest to the actual number.

TWO TICKY TALES   (PAGE 49)

Overview Children use cows, giraffes, crocodiles, rhinos, and camels to solve a story problem involving number concepts, addition, and subtraction. Let children respond to the picture on the activity page and read the story with them. Make sure children understand the concept of trading. You might use as an example giving someone five pennies for a nickel. Ask children for other examples.

Before Since this story is reminiscent of "Jack and the Beanstalk" and other traditional fairy tales, you might want to have children talk about fairy tales before they look at the activity page.

© 1995 Cuisenaire Company

After As part of a discussion, use key questions such as these:
- How many animals did Ticky have after he traded 1 cow for 2 giraffes? For 3 crocodiles? For 4 rhinos? For 5 camels?
- Is this more or fewer cows than the number of cows Ticky started with?
- Why would Ticky's mother be upset by what she saw?

Going Further Children may enjoy drawing a picture showing how Ticky's mother looked when she saw all of the animals. Older children also can illustrate their own Ticky Tale and put it in a class "Ticky Tales" file for classmates to read and solve using animal pieces.

© 1995 Cuisenaire Company

The Far North

Read the story.
Add animals to show what happens.

"I see them," whispered the girl
to her mother.

"What do you see, my child?"
asked the mother in a soft voice.

"I see 2 little polar bears coming,"
whispered the girl.

"They must be looking for their mother."

"I see 2 more big seals swimming to the rock.
There are 2 more baby seals with them."

How many animals are there altogether?
How did you find out?

Make up another story.
Put animals in the picture to show what happens.

© 1995 Cuisenaire Company

Animal Bazaar

Help to tell the story.

Kumar and his father buy and sell animals.
One morning, they had 5 big elephants,
4 little elephants, 2 small horses,
1 big camel, and 2 little camels.

Add animals to the picture.
Show how many there were in the morning.

Kumar's father went for lunch. Kumar sold 1 big elephant,
2 little elephants, 1 small horse, and 1 little camel.

When Kumar's father came back, he said,
"You did very well, my son."

Take animals away from the picture to show what happened.
How many animals are left?

Now change the story.
Use animal pieces to show what happens.

© 1995 Cuisenaire Company

The Animal Kingdom

All the animals lived as friends
in a make-believe kingdom.

1 monkey

2 lions

3 elephants

4 giraffes

5 camels

6 sheep

7 horses

8 pigs

How many animals are there altogether?
Line up your animals on the page to find out.

One day, the monkey, some giraffes, and some horses
ran off to join the circus.

Decide how many giraffes and horses you want to remove.
Take away that number of animals.
Then change places with a partner.

How many giraffes and horses did your partner take away?
Talk with your partner about how you know.

Change the story.
Use animal pieces to show what happens.

© 1995 Cuisenaire Company

Two Ticky Tales

Help to tell the story.
Add or take away animals.

Ticky's mother told him to buy 4 cows.
"We are poor," she said.
"We can sell the milk.
I wish we could buy more cows,
but there isn't enough money."

Ticky bought 4 cows.
Then a man said he would trade
2 giraffes for 1 cow.
"Good," thought Ticky.
"More animals. My mother will be so
pleased."

Then Ticky traded
1 cow for 3 crocodiles
1 cow for 4 rhinos
1 cow for 5 camels.

After that, Ticky went home.
"Eeek!" screamed Ticky's mother when
she saw him.

What did she see?

Ticky's mother is not happy.
How can Ticky fix it?
Use the animals to make up
another Ticky Tale.

© 1995 Cuisenaire Company

Finding Strategies with Animals

A strategy can be thought of as a problem-solving maneuver. Manipulating the animal pieces helps children to think strategically. In attempting to solve problems, they can try out their tactics in a three-dimensional way—a more vivid approach than trying to visualize strategies without "props." Young children, especially, are visual and literal, and a situation becomes real as they act it out by moving animals around. With the animals, children can readily try different methods to find the one that works best.

There are usually several different strategies that can solve the same problem. Encourage children to discuss and then try their own way with a partner or in a group. Have the class share its strategies and discuss which seem to work the best or make the most sense for the situation.

CROCODILE (PAGE 54)

Overview Children play a game in which the players remove animal pieces, and the player who takes the next to the last piece wins.

Before Ask children to talk about games they play that have winners and losers. Focus on one or two popular games and ask children whether there are things they do to try to win. Explain that often we can discover different ways to play games or solve problems. Sometimes, some ways are better than others for helping us win or solve our problem.

After Invite different children or groups to share and compare any strategies they used. As part of the discussion, use key questions such as these:
- Can you win every time if you use your strategy? Why or why not?
- How would the game change if you had nine animals and a crocodile?

Going Further You may want children to try out their new version of the game by changing partners and playing again.

BARNYARD ROUNDUP (PAGE 55)

Overview Partners play a game in which they plan the number of animals to pick up each turn in order to take the last remaining animal.

Before Point out that this game is both like and different from the Crocodile game. After reading the directions, invite children to tell how. You may want children to recall some of the steps and strategies they have already used. Have children speculate about whether any of these will work here, and why or why not.

After Ask children what (if any) similarities or differences they noticed between the strategy for this game and the crocodile game.

As part of the discussion, use key questions such as these:
- How many animals did you take away most of the time?
- Does it matter how many you pick up in the beginning of the game? Towards the end of the game?
- Does it matter if you go first? Last?

© 1995 Cuisenaire Company

Going Further As an interesting variation to the game, challenge children to write addition and/or subtraction problems before each move.

THE MONKEY HOP   (PAGE 56)

Overview Children use a large and a small monkey to act out a story and solve a number-pattern problem.

Before Since children will be working with number patterns, they may benefit from some review of skip counting by 2s and 3s. Before they begin, have children look over the activity page and consider how they could use their monkey pieces to solve the problem, since the pieces don't stand easily.

After During the discussion about which strategies seem best, guide children to see that different strategies can work to solve the same problem. Some possible strategies to solve this problem are numbering the steps from 1-12 and making a list to record which steps each monkey stepped on; acting out the problem with monkeys; and using two colors of crayons to show the monkeys' paths. Both monkeys should have landed on steps 6 and 12 and skipped over steps 1, 5, 7, and 11.

Going Further Some children may enjoy recording the monkey story in their journals with words, pictures, or both. Challenge others to extend the problem to 20 stairs.

JUNGLE PARADE   (PAGE 57)

Overview Children work backwards to solve a problem involving sorting and classifying, and then find possible combinations of three animals.

Before Remind children of previous sorting and classifying activities. Tell them that this problem has two steps to solve. One involves sorting and classifying. Suggest that students make three loops to organize their thinking as they work. Tell children to record all the combinations of three animals using the animal cutouts on pages 69 and 71.

After Have various children identify the three groups in which they decided the lion, the hippo, and the monkey belong. Some of the ways to classify the three animals are as animals with short tails, long tails, or no tails; animals that live in water, on the ground, or in the trees; animals that are brown and pink, tan and white, and all others. Ask children to give the different combinations they found for the three leaders.

THE GREAT RACE   (PAGE 58)

Overview Children use logical thinking to follow clues, act out a problem, and create a new problem.

Before Read the page with the children. Ask them how the animals might help them to solve this problem. Soon after that, have children begin working.

After Ask children to describe their strategies and the different order of animals they may have tried. Children may record in their journals their reasoning about the order in which the four animals finished the race.

Give children time to trade and solve their problems with classmates.

© 1995 Cuisenaire Company

BACK IN THE BARNYARD   (PAGE 59)

Overview Children use logical reasoning to solve an addition and subtraction problem.

Before Ask children to listen carefully as you read the activity page aloud. Before solving the problem, have children identify the question they need to answer.

After As part of a discussion, use key questions such as these:
- What did you need to find out before you could answer the question?
- How did you go about solving the problem?

LIONS AND ELEPHANTS   (PAGE 60)

Overview Pairs of children plan the moves in this strategy game in order to block their opponents' pieces.

Before Review the rules of the game very carefully, possibly demonstrating on an overhead projector how to play so that children master the moves they can and cannot make. Make sure they understand these rules: When moving into the center, a player can only move a lion that is next to an elephant or an elephant that is next to a lion, and a player is blocked when there is no empty space next to his or her animals, an animal is already in the center, or no animal is next to the other kind to move.

After Have children share strategies. Talk about how many moves it took until the game was over each time.

BUILDING FENCES   (PAGE 61)

Overview Children experiment with area and perimeter as they create closed figures with eight straws and look for the figure with the greatest area.

Before Give each child or pair of children three nonbendable straws and have them cut the straws into thirds. (Or you may prefer precutting the straws yourself.) If you like, children can use very small bits of clay to temporarily hold arrangements in place. Suggest that children draw each figure and the number of animals that fit before altering the figure.

After Let children talk about the frustrations of standing up a lot of animals close together in a closed space. Invite children to talk about what they did and what they found out. Ask casually why children think the space inside the fence can change even though they use the same number of straws. Call on several children to hold up their drawings of the straw arrangement that held the most animals, the next most, and so on.

Going Further As an interesting variation, have children try the same activity using uncut straws or toothpicks. Discuss how the answers change. Children can also write addition and/or subtraction problems before each move.

© 1995 Cuisenaire Company

Crocodile

Play the Crocodile game with a partner.
Put out 1 crocodile and 12 other animals.

Take turns.
Pick up and keep 1 or 2 animals each turn.
But do *not* pick up the crocodile!

The player who doesn't pick up the crocodile
wins the game.

Play the game four or five more times.
Figure out what you need to do so that
you can win.

How could you change the game?

Finding Strategies ANIMAL MATH
© 1995 Cuisenaire Company

Barnyard Roundup

Play this game with a partner.
Set up animals as you see them below.
Take turns.
Remove 1, 2, or 3 animals each turn.
The animals must be in the same row or column.

Try to plan ahead.
Think about the number of animals you will take.
Whoever takes the last animal wins the game.

Play the game again with more animals.

How else could you change the game?

© 1995 Cuisenaire Company

The Monkey Hop

Find a way to solve this problem.

A big monkey and a little monkey
want to hop up 12 steps.

The little monkey takes
2 steps in one hop.
The big monkey takes
3 steps in one hop.

Which steps do both
monkeys land on?

Which steps do both
monkeys skip over?

Which monkey gets
there first?

Talk with classmates about how they worked.
Talk about any number patterns you see.

Finding Strategies   ANIMAL MATH
© 1995 Cuisenaire Company

Jungle Parade

Work with a partner.
Use all the wild animals.
Find a way to solve the problem.

The Hippo King called out,
"We need 3 leaders for the
Jungle Parade. I want each
animal to feel there is one leader
for him or her."

"Choose me, choose me,"cried all
the animals.

"We'll see," said the Hippo King.
"First I have to sort you all into 3 groups."
So that's what he did.

Then he chose one animal from each group.
He chose a lion, a hippo, and a monkey.
"These animals will lead our parade."

How do you think the Hippo King
sorted the animals?
Try it with your animals.

Now there were 3 good leaders.
But who would go first?
Who would go second? Who would go third?
The Hippo King wanted to see which
order looked best.

How many different ways can you
order the 3 leaders?

© 1995 Cuisenaire Company

The Great Race

Use animals to solve this problem.

A giraffe, a rhino, a camel, and an elephant are having a race.
- The elephant is usually the slowest animal. But today he wins the race.
- The giraffe runs faster than the rhino, but more slowly than the camel.

Show how the 4 runners looked just before the race ended.

Make up another problem about an animal race.
First plan out who should win and how the other runners will do.
Trade problems with a classmate.

© 1995 Cuisenaire Company

Back in the Barnyard

Use animals to solve this problem.

The farmer had 7 cows, 3 sheep, 4 horses, and 6 pigs.
On Monday someone left the barnyard gate open.
All the animals got out.
The farmer just waited.

On Tuesday none of the animals came back.
On Wednesday some of them came back.
By Thursday 10 animals were still in the woods.
They all came back on Friday.
Then the farmer closed the gate.

How many animals came back on Wednesday?
What strategies can you use to
answer the question?

Use more animals to tell a barnyard story.
Plan your story with or without animal pieces.

Ask a classmate to solve the problem in your story.

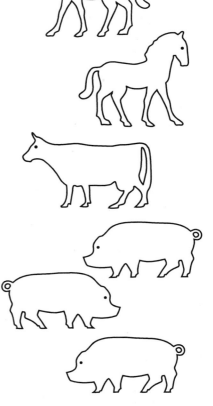

© 1995 Cuisenaire Company

Lions and Elephants

Play this game with a partner.
Put lions and elephants on their pictures.
Decide who will move lions and
who will move elephants.
Decide who goes first.
That player moves 1 animal to the circle in the middle.

Partners take turns moving animals around the board.

Whoever stays in the game longest wins.

Here are the ways you can move.

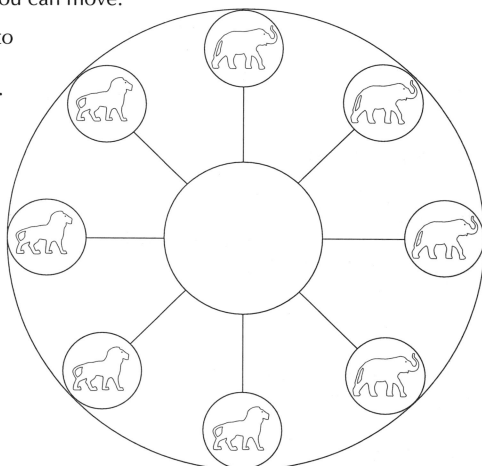

- If the circle next to
  1 of your animals
  is empty, go there.

- If 1 of your
  animals is next
  to 1 of your
  partner's
  animals,
  go to the
  middle.

- If you have
  an animal
  in the middle,
  move to any
  empty space.

Play again. How can you plan your moves to help you win?

Finding Strategies   ANIMAL MATH

© 1995 Cuisenaire Company

Building Fences

Start with 3 drinking straws.
Cut each one into 3 pieces.
Try to make all the pieces the same length.
Take away 1 piece.
How many pieces will you have left for building fences?

Follow these steps.

1. Make a fence like this on the table.
   Make sure the ends touch.

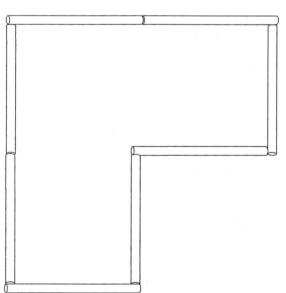

2. Stand up as many big animals as you
   can inside the fence.

3. Count the animals that fit.

4. Move the straws around
   so that you can fit in more animals.
   Count the animals that fit.
   Draw your fence designs.

5. Make as many different fences as you can
   with 8 straw pieces.
   Count the number of animals that fit each time.
   Show all your designs.

What fence design will hold the most little animals?

© 1995 Cuisenaire Company

Telling More Math Stories

This cluster introduces more stories involving addition and subtraction, logical thinking, nonroutine and open-ended problems, and basic multiplication and division concepts. Children are encouraged to use the animal pieces as they think creatively and develop stories. They must decide on strategies, use computation or other methods to find a solution, and share and compare results with others.

As with the earlier cluster of math stories, you may want to read all the stories aloud while children follow along. Or, you may want to give children an opportunity to read some of the stories themselves. Encourage journal writing and other methods of recording throughout.

AFRICAN NIGHT   (PAGE 65)

Overview Children apply logic while manipulating animals in an addition, subtraction, and one-to-one matching problem.

Before To introduce the story, children can locate Africa on a wall map. Explain that Africa is made up of many countries and has mountains, deserts, and jungles. Point out that today's story takes place somewhere in Africa where rhinos, monkeys, giraffes, and hippos all live together. Choose volunteers to read the story aloud while other children follow along silently. Take time for children to talk about the illustration and link it to the story.

After As a part of a discussion, use key questions such as these:
- How many animals were at the watering hole to start? How did you find out?
- How many monkeys were watching from up in the tree? How do you know this?

Allow children time to express their strategies in their own ways. Establish that after taking away the animals that left, children could count the number remaining and thus know how many monkeys there were.

Going Further As an extension, children could investigate the eating habits of real African jungle animals to find out what they eat.

THE MAGIC JAR   (PAGE 66)

Overview Children solve a problem involving basic addition and multiplication skills by doubling the numbers 1-6.

Before In preparation for this activity, have children cut out as many copies of the animal pictures from pages 69 and 71 as needed in conjunction with the animal pieces. Children can work partly on the activity page and partly on another paper or on the table.

Invite comments and speculation about the pictures. Then give various children a turn at reading the story aloud.

After As part of a discussion, use key questions such as these:
- What happened when the king went into the jar? How do you know that?
- If the king put in 10 giraffes, how could you find out how many would come out?

© 1995 Cuisenaire Company

- How many sheep went into the jar? How many came out? What addition fact tells what happened? What multiplication fact tells what happened?

Going Further Encourage children to use the animal pieces and pictures to show greater animal doubles, using the numbers 7-12. Challenge children to record an addition or multiplication problem to express what they have done.

THE BARNYARD MYSTERY   (PAGE 67)

Overview Children observe and use details from a barnyard scene to create a mystery story involving numbers.

Before Have children examine the picture on the activity page and talk about it. Go over the directions. Make sure children understand that everyone needs to get ideas for his or her own number story. Encourage creativity and allow problems to come naturally out of playing with the animals on the barnyard picture. If necessary for your group, ask children before they begin to share their ideas about the barnyard scene: What is happening to the different animals and what could happen next?

After Allow as many children as possible to share their stories and their solutions, taking time to recognize any math involved in the situations. This process may extend over several periods.

Going Further Children can draw pictures such as the barnyard scene and make up problem situations about them.

CROSSING THE RIVER   (PAGE 68)

Overview In order to tell a story, children have to meet the challenging terms of a logic problem that involves deciding how many animals must be in a group.

Before To arouse children's interest, discuss any experiences children may have had going out on a lake or river in a rowboat. Look at the picture together. Make sure children realize that they will place their animals in the boat as they work to solve the problem.

After Ask children to share their solutions and strategies. (In order to have the least number of trips, the animals would have to make four trips.) Invite a few children to read their stories to the class.

© 1995 Cuisenaire Company

African Night

Help to tell the first part of the story.
Put more animals in the picture.

It was a beautiful moonlit night.
The animals came to the watering hole.
There were 4 rhinos, 2 giraffes, and 3 hippos.
The animals drank the water.
They were very thirsty.
Some monkeys watched from up in a tree.

Read the rest of the story.
Fix the picture so that it shows the ending.

Three rhinos, 1 giraffe, and 1 hippo went away
to take a nap.
Just enough animals were left to give
each monkey a ride.
You can see the monkeys in the tree.

How many monkeys do you see?

Make up an African Night story of your own.
Put animals in the picture.

© 1995 Cuisenaire Company

The Magic Jar

Read the story.
Then use animals and pictures to solve the problem.

Once upon a time in China,
there lived a tricky Monkey King.
The Monkey King had a magic jar.
When he put things into the jar,
something funny happened.

The Monkey King put in

1 bear and out came 2.
2 lions and out came 4.
3 pigs and out came 6.
4 sheep and out came 8.
5 cows and out came 10.
6 horses and out came 12.

One day the people said,
"We want to have more
animals. Let us use your jar."
The King said no. So the
people chased him around.
The King jumped into his jar to get away.
How many Kings do you suppose
came out of the jar?

What was the jar's magic trick?
Remember to use animals and pictures to answer this question.
Tell what happened next in the story.

© 1995 Cuisenaire Company

The Barnyard Mystery

Look at the picture. Use it to make up
a math mystery.
Use your animals to plan your story.
Put one or two number questions in it.

Tell your story to a classmate.
He or she can use animals to
solve your mystery.

© 1995 Cuisenaire Company

Crossing the River

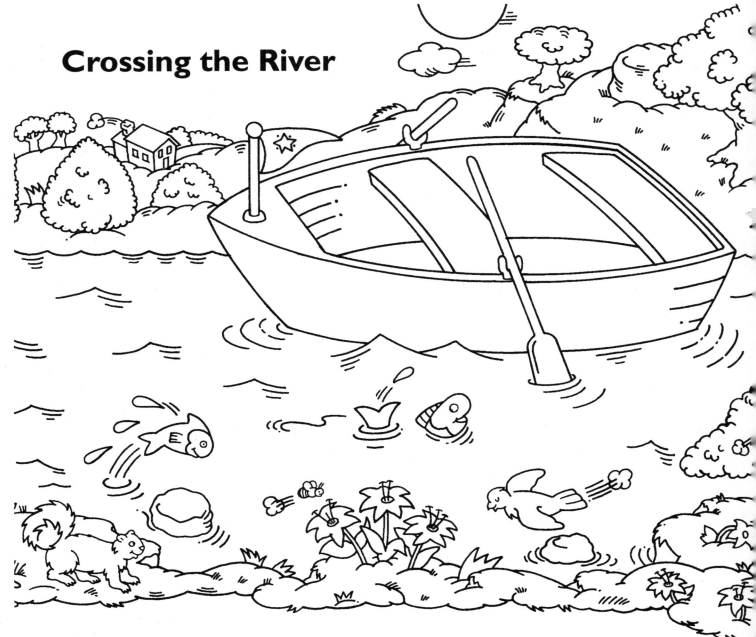

Look at the picture.
Suppose that 10 of your animals needed to cross the river in a boat.

There is only 1 boat.
The boat holds up to 4 animals.
One animal needs to row back each time.

Make up a story about it.

First use your animals to find out how many trips it will take.

© 1995 Cuisenaire Company

© 1995 Cuisenaire Company

© 1995 Cuisenaire Company